The Collected Poetry

Dorthy Parker

THE MODERN LIBRARY
OF THE WORLD'S BEST BOOKS

THE COLLECTED POETRY

of

DOROTHY PARKER

THE
COLLECTED
POETRY
OF
DOROTHY
PARKER

THE MODERN LIBRARY · NEW YORK

THE PRESIDENCY BOOK SUPPLIES
8-C. PYCROFT'S ROAD. TRIPLICANE. MADRAS 5

TO

FRANKLIN PIERCE ADAMS

CONTENTS

ENOUGH ROPE

[viii]

ENOUGH
ROPE

THRENODY

Lilacs blossom just as sweet
Now my heart is shattered.
If I bowled it down the street,
Who's to say it mattered?
If there's one that rode away
What would I be missing?
Lips that taste of tears, they say,
Are the best for kissing.

Eyes that watch the morning star
Seem a little brighter;
Arms held out to darkness are
Usually whiter.
Shall I bar the strolling guest,
Bind my brow with willow,
When, they say, the empty breast
Is the softer pillow?

That a heart falls tinkling down,
Never think it ceases.
Every likely lad in town
Gathers up the pieces.
If there's one gone whistling by
Would I let it grieve me?
Let him wonder if I lie;
Let him half believe me.

THE SMALL HOURS

No more my little song comes back;
　And now of nights I lay
My head on down, to watch the black
　And wait the unfailing gray.

Oh, sad are winter nights, and slow;
　And sad's a song that's dumb;
And sad it is to lie and know
　Another dawn will come.

THE FALSE FRIENDS

They laid their hands upon my head,
They stroked my cheek and brow;
And time could heal a hurt, they said,
And time could dim a vow.

And they were pitiful and mild
Who whispered to me then.
"The heart that breaks in April, child,
Will mend in May again."

Oh, many a mended heart they knew,
So old they were, and wise.
And little did they have to do
To come to me with lies!

Who flings me silly talk of May
Shall meet a bitter soul;
For June was nearly spent away
Before my heart was whole.

THE TRIFLER

Death's the lover that I'd be taking;
  Wild and fickle and fierce is he.
Small's his care if my heart be breaking—
  Gay young Death would have none of me.

Hear them clack of my haste to greet him!
  No one other my mouth had kissed.
I had dressed me in silk to meet him—
  False young Death would not hold the tryst.

Slow's the blood that was quick and stormy,
  Smooth and cold is the bridal bed;
I must wait till he whistles for me—
  Proud young Death would not turn his head.

I must wait till my breast is wilted,
  I must wait till my back is bowed,
I must rock in the corner, jilted—
  Death went galloping down the road.

Gone's my heart with a trifling rover.
  Fine he was in the game he played—
Kissed, and promised, and threw me over,
  And rode away with a prettier maid.

A VERY SHORT SONG

Once, when I was young and true,
    Someone left me sad—
Broke my brittle heart in two;
    And that is very bad.

Love is for unlucky folk,
    Love is but a curse.
Once there was a heart I broke;
    And that, I think, is worse.

A WELL-WORN STORY

In April, in April,
My one love came along,
And I ran the slope of my high hill
To follow a thread of song.

His eyes were hard as porphyry
With looking on cruel lands;
His voice went slipping over me
Like terrible silver hands.

Together we trod the secret lane
And walked the muttering town.
I wore my heart like a wet, red stain
On the breast of a velvet gown.

In April, in April,
My love went whistling by,
And I stumbled here to my high hill
Along the way of a lie.

Now what should I do in this place
But sit and count the chimes,
And splash cold water on my face
And spoil a page with rhymes?

CONVALESCENT

How shall I wail, that wasn't meant for weeping?
Love has run and left me, oh, what then?
Dream, then, I must, who never can be sleeping;
What if I should meet Love, once again?

What if I met him, walking on the highway?
Let him see how lightly I should care.
He'd travel his way, I would follow my way;
Hum a little song, and pass him there.

What if at night, beneath a sky of ashes,
He should seek my doorstep, pale with need?
There could he lie, and dry would be my lashes;
Let him stop his noise, and let me read.

Oh, but I'm gay, that's better off without him;
Would he'd come and see me, laughing here.
Lord! Don't I know I'd have my arms about him,
Crying to him, "Oh, come in, my dear!"

THE DARK GIRL'S RHYME

Who was there had seen us
  Wouldn't bid him run?
Heavy lay between us
  All our sires had done.

There he was, a-springing
  Of a pious race,
Setting hags a-swinging
  In a market-place;

Sowing turnips over
  Where the poppies lay;
Looking past the clover,
  Adding up the hay;

Shouting through the Spring song,
  Clumping down the sod;
Toadying, in sing-song,
  To a crabbèd god.

There I was, that came of
  Folk of mud and flame—
I that had my name of
  Them without a name.

Up and down a mountain
  Streeled my silly stock;
Passing by a fountain,
  Wringing at a rock;

Devil-gotten sinners,
　　Throwing back their heads;
Fiddling for their dinners,
　　Kissing for their beds.

Not a one had seen us
　　Wouldn't help him flee.
Angry ran between us
　　Blood of him and me.

How shall I be mating
　　Who have looked above—
Living for a hating,
　　Dying of a love?

EPITAPH

The first time I died, I walked my ways;
I followed the file of limping days.

I held me tall, with my head flung up,
But I dared not look on the new moon's cup.

I dared not look on the sweet young rain,
And between my ribs was a gleaming pain.

The next time I died, they laid me deep.
They spoke worn words to hallow my sleep.

They tossed me petals, they wreathed me fern,
They weighted me down with a marble urn.

And I lie here warm, and I lie here dry,
And watch the worms slip by, slip by.

LIGHT OF LOVE

Joy stayed with me a night—
Young and free and fair—
And in the morning light
He left me there.

Then Sorrow came to stay,
And lay upon my breast;
He walked with me in the day,
And knew me best.

I'll never be a bride,
Nor yet celibate,
So I'm living now with Pride—
A cold bedmate.

He must not hear nor see,
Nor could he forgive
That Sorrow still visits me
Each day I live.

WAIL

Love has gone a-rocketing.
  That is not the worst;
I could do without the thing,
  And not be the first.

Joy has gone the way it came.
  That is nothing new;
I could get along the same—
  Many people do.

Dig for me the narrow bed,
  Now I am bereft.
All my pretty hates are dead,
  And what have I left?

THE SATIN DRESS

Needle, needle, dip and dart,
Thrusting up and down,
Where's the man could ease a heart
Like a satin gown?

See the stitches curve and crawl
Round the cunning seams—
Patterns thin and sweet and small
As a lady's dreams.

Wantons go in bright brocades;
Brides in organdie;
Gingham's for the plighted maid;
Satin's for the free!

Wool's to line a miser's chest;
Crape's to calm the old;
Velvet hides an empty breast;
Satin's for the bold!

Lawn is for a bishop's yoke;
Linen's for a nun;
Satin is for wiser folk—
Would the dress were done!

Satin glows in candlelight—
Satin's for the proud!
They will say who watch at night,
"What a fine shroud!"

SOMEBODY'S SONG

This is what I vow:
He shall have my heart to keep;
Sweetly will we stir and sleep,
     All the years, as now.
Swift the measured sands may run;
Love like this is never done;
He and I are welded one:
     This is what I vow.

This is what I pray:
Keep him by me tenderly;
Keep him sweet in pride of me,
     Ever and a day;
Keep me from the old distress;
Let me, for our happiness,
Be the one to love the less:
     This is what I pray.

This is what I know:
Lovers' oaths are thin as rain;
Love's a harbinger of pain—
     Would it were not so!
Ever is my heart a-thirst,
Ever is my love accurst;
He is neither last nor first:
     This is what I know.

ANECDOTE

So silent I when Love was by
   He yawned, and turned away;
But Sorrow clings to my apron-strings,
   I have so much to say.

BRAGGART

The days will rally, wreathing
Their crazy tarantelle;
And you must go on breathing,
But I'll be safe in hell.

Like January weather,
The years will bite and smart,
And pull your bones together
To wrap your chattering heart.

The pretty stuff you're made of
Will crack and crease and dry.
The thing you are afraid of
Will look from every eye.

You will go faltering after
The bright, imperious line,
And split your throat on laughter,
And burn your eyes with brine.

You will be frail and musty
With peering, furtive head,
Whilst I am young and lusty
Among the roaring dead.

EPITAPH FOR A DARLING LADY

All her hours were yellow sands,
Blown in foolish whorls and tassels;
Slipping warmly through her hands;
Patted into little castles.

Shiny day on shiny day
Tumbled in a rainbow clutter,
As she flipped them all away,
Sent them spinning down the gutter.

Leave for her a red young rose,
Go your way, and save your pity;
She is happy, for she knows
That her dust is very pretty.

A MUCH TOO UNFORTUNATE LADY

He will love you presently
If you be the way you be.
Send your heart a-skittering,
He will stoop, and lift the thing.
Be your dreams as thread, to tease
Into patterns he shall please.
Let him see your passion is
Ever tenderer than his. . . .
Go and bless your star above,
Thus are you, and thus is Love.

He will leave you white with woe,
If you go the way you go.
If your dreams were thread to weave,
He will pluck them from his sleeve.
If your heart had come to rest,
He will flick it from his breast.
Tender though the love he bore,
You had loved a little more. . . .
Lady, go and curse your star,
Thus Love is, and thus you are.

PATHS

I shall tread, another year,
　　Ways I walked with Grief,
Past the dry, ungarnered ear
　　And the brittle leaf.

I shall stand, a year apart,
　　Wondering, and shy,
Thinking, "Here she broke her heart;
　　Here she pled to die."

I shall hear the pheasants call,
　　And the raucous geese;
Down these ways, another Fall,
　　I shall walk with Peace.

But the pretty path I trod
　　Hand-in-hand with Love—
Underfoot, the nascent sod,
　　Brave young boughs above,

And the stripes of ribbon grass
　　By the curling way—
I shall never dare to pass
　　To my dying day.

HEARTHSIDE

Half across the world from me
Lie the lands I'll never see—
I, whose longing lives and dies
Where a ship has sailed away;
I, that never close my eyes
But to look upon Cathay.

Things I may not know nor tell
Wait, where older waters swell;
Ways that flowered at Sappho's tread,
Winds that sighed in Homer's strings,
Vibrant with the singing dead,
Golden with the dust of wings.

Under deeper skies than mine,
Quiet valleys dip and shine.
Where their tender grasses heal
Ancient scars of trench and tomb
I shall never walk; nor kneel
Where the bones of poets bloom.

If I seek a lovelier part,
Where I travel goes my heart;
Where I stray my thought must go;
With me wanders my desire.
Best to sit and watch the snow,
Turn the lock, and poke the fire.

THE NEW LOVE

If it shine or if it rain,
    Little will I care or know.
Days, like drops upon a pane,
    Slip, and join, and go.

At my door's another lad;
    Here's his flower in my hair
If he see me pale and sad,
    Will he see me fair?

I sit looking at the floor.
    Little will I think or say
If he seek another door;
    Even if he stay.

RAINY NIGHT

Ghosts of all my lovely sins,
   Who attend too well my pillow,
Gay the wanton rain begins;
   Hide the limp and tearful willow,

Turn aside your eyes and ears,
   Trail away your robes of sorrow.
You shall have my further years—
   You shall walk with me tomorrow.

I am sister to the rain;
   Fey and sudden and unholy,
Petulant at the windowpane,
   Quickly lost, remembered slowly.

I have lived with shades, a shade;
   I am hung with graveyard flowers.
Let me be tonight arrayed
   In the silver of the showers.

Every fragile thing shall rust;
   When another April passes
I may be a furry dust,
   Sifting through the brittle grasses.

All sweet sins shall be forgot;
   Who will live to tell their siring?
Hear me now, nor let me rot
   Wistful still, and still aspiring.

Ghosts of dear temptations, heed;
   I am frail, be you forgiving.
See you not that I have need
   To be living with the living?

Sail, tonight, the Styx's breast;
   Glide among the dim processions
Of the exquisite unblest,
   Spirits of my shared transgressions.

Roam with young Persephone,
   Plucking poppies for your slumber . .
With the morrow, there shall be
   One more wraith among your number.

FOR A SAD LADY

And let her loves, when she is dead,
  Write this above her bones:
"No more she lives to give us bread
  Who asked her only stones."

RECURRENCE

We shall have our little day.
Take my hand and travel still
Round and round the little way,
Up and down the little hill.

It is good to love again;
Scan the renovated skies,
Dip and drive the idling pen,
Sweetly tint the paling lies.

Trace the dripping, piercèd heart,
Speak the fair, insistent verse,
Vow to God, and slip apart,
Little better, little worse.

Would we need not know before
How shall end this prettiness;
One of us must love the more,
One of us shall love the less.

Thus it is, and so it goes;
We shall have our day, my dear.
Where, unwilling, dies the rose
Buds the new, another year.

STORY OF MRS. W——

My garden blossoms pink and white,
   A place of decorous murmuring,
Where I am safe from August night
   And cannot feel the knife of Spring.

And I may walk the pretty place
   Before the curtsying hollyhocks
And laundered daisies, round of face—
   Good little girls, in party frocks.

My trees are amiably arrayed
   In pattern on the dappled sky,
And I may sit in filtered shade
   And watch the tidy years go by.

And I may amble pleasantly
   And hear my neighbors list their bones
And click my tongue in sympathy,
   And count the cracks in paving-stones.

My door is grave in oaken strength,
   The cool of linen calms my bed,
And there at night I stretch my length
   And envy no one but the dead.

THE DRAMATISTS

A string of shiny days we had,
   A spotless sky, a yellow sun;
And neither you nor I was sad
   When that was through and done.

But when, one day, a boy comes by
   And pleads me with your happiest vow.
"There was a lad I knew___" I'll sigh;
   "I do not know him now."

And when another girl shall pass
   And speak a little name I said,
Then you will say, "There was a lass—
   I wonder is she dead."

And each of us will sigh, and start
   A-talking of a faded year,
And lay a hand above a heart,
   And dry a pretty tear.

AUGUST

When my eyes are weeds,
And my lips are petals, spinning
Down the wind that has beginning
Where the crumpled beeches start
In a fringe of salty reeds;
When my arms are elder-bushes,
And the rangy lilac pushes
Upward, upward through my heart;

Summer, do your worst!
Light your tinsel moon, and call on
Your performing stars to fall on
Headlong through your paper sky;
Nevermore shall I be cursed
By a flushed and amorous slattern,
With her dusty laces' pattern
Trailing, as she straggles by.

THE WHITE LADY

I cannot rest, I cannot rest
　　In strait and shiny wood,
My woven hands upon my breast—
　　The dead are all so good!

The earth is cool across their eyes;
　　They lie there quietly.
But I am neither old nor wise;
　　They do not welcome me.

Where never I walked alone before,
　　I wander in the weeds;
And people scream and bar the door,
　　And rattle at their beads.

We cannot rest, we never rest
　　Within a narrow bed
Who still must love the living best—
　　Who hate the drowsy dead!

I KNOW I HAVE BEEN HAPPIEST

I know I have been happiest at your side;
But what is done, is done, and all's to be.
And small the good, to linger dolefully—
Gayly it lived, and gallantly it died.
I will not make you songs of hearts denied,
And you, being man, would have no tears of me,
And should I offer you fidelity,
You'd be, I think, a little terrified.

Yet this the need of woman, this her curse:
To range her little gifts, and give, and give,
Because the throb of giving's sweet to bear.
To you, who never begged me vows or verse.
My gift shall be my absence, while I live;
But after that, my dear, I cannot swear.

TESTAMENT

Oh, let it be a night of lyric rain
And singing breezes, when my bell is tolled.
I have so loved the rain that I would hold
Last in my ears its friendly, dim refrain.
I shall lie cool and quiet, who have lain
Fevered, and watched the book of day unfold.
Death will not see me flinch; the heart is bold
That pain has made incapable of pain.

Kinder the busy worms than ever love;
It will be peace to lie there, empty-eyed,
My bed made secret by the leveling showers,
My breast replenishing the weeds above.
And you will say of me, "Then has she died?
Perhaps I should have sent a spray of flowers."

I SHALL COME BACK

I shall come back without fanfaronade
Of wailing wind and graveyard panoply;
But, trembling, slip from cool Eternity—
A mild and most bewildered little shade.
I shall not make sepulchral midnight raid,
But softly come where I had longed to be
In April twilight's unsung melody,
And I, not you, shall be the one afraid.

Strange, that from lovely dreamings of the dead
I shall come back to you, who hurt me most.
You may not feel my hand upon your head,
I'll be so new and inexpert a ghost.
Perhaps you will not know that I am near—
And that will break my ghostly heart, my dear.

CONDOLENCE

They hurried here, as soon as you had died,
Their faces damp with haste and sympathy,
And pressed my hand in theirs, and smoothed my knee,
And clicked their tongues, and watched me, mournful-
     eyed.
Gently they told me of that Other Side—
How, even then, you waited there for me,
And what ecstatic meeting ours would be.
Moved by the lovely tale, they broke, and cried.

And when I smiled, they told me I was brave,
And they rejoiced that I was comforted,
And left, to tell of all the help they gave.
But I had smiled to think how you, the dead,
So curiously preoccupied and grave,
Would laugh, could you have heard the things they said.

THE IMMORTALS

If you should sail for Trebizond, or die,
Or cry another name in your first sleep,
Or see me board a train, and fail to sigh,
Appropriately, I'd clutch my breast and weep.
And you, if I should wander through the door,
Or sin, or seek a nunnery, or save
My lips and give my cheek, would tread the floor
And aptly mention poison and the grave.

Therefore the mooning world is gratified,
Quoting how prettily we sigh and swear;
And you and I, correctly side by side,
Shall live as lovers when our bones are bare;
And though we lie forever enemies,
Shall rank with Abélard and Héloïse.

A PORTRAIT

Because my love is quick to come and go—
A little here, and then a little there—
What use are any words of mine to swear
My heart is stubborn, and my spirit slow
Of weathering the drip and drive of woe?
What is my oath, when you have but to bare
My little, easy loves; and I can dare
Only to shrug, and answer, "They are so"?

You do not know how heavy a heart it is
That hangs about my neck—a clumsy stone
Cut with a birth, a death, a bridal-day.
Each time I love, I find it still my own,
Who take it, now to that lad, now to this,
Seeking to give the wretched thing away.

PORTRAIT OF THE ARTIST

Oh, lead me to a quiet cell
   Where never footfall rankles,
And bar the window passing well,
   And gyve my wrists and ankles.

Oh, wrap my eyes with linen fair,
   With hempen cord go bind me,
And, of your mercy, leave me there,
   Nor tell them where to find me.

Oh, lock the portal as you go,
   And see its bolts be double. . . .
Come back in half an hour or so,
   And I will be in trouble.

CHANT FOR DARK HOURS

Some men, some men
Cannot pass a
Book shop.
(Lady, make your mind up, and wait your life away.)

Some men, some men
Cannot pass a
Crap game.
(He said he'd come at moonrise, and here's another day!)

Some men, some men
Cannot pass a
Bar-room.
(Wait about, and hang about, and that's the way it goes.)

Some men, some men
Cannot pass a
Woman.
(Heaven never send me another one of those!)

Some men, some men
Cannot pass a
Golf course.
(Read a book, and sew a seam, and slumber if you can.)

Some men, some men
Cannot pass a
Haberdasher's.
(All your life you wait around for some damn man!)

UNFORTUNATE COINCIDENCE

By the time you swear you're his,
  Shivering and sighing,
And he vows his passion is
  Infinite, undying—
Lady, make a note of this:
  One of you is lying.

INVENTORY

Four be the things I am wiser to know:
Idleness, sorrow, a friend, and a foe.

Four be the things I'd been better without:
Love, curiosity, freckles, and doubt.

Three be the things I shall never attain:
Envy, content, and sufficient champagne.

Three be the things I shall have till I die:
Laughter and hope and a sock in the eye.

NOW AT LIBERTY

Little white love, your way you've taken;
　Now I am left alone, alone.
Little white love, my heart's forsaken.
　(Whom shall I get by telephone?)
Well do I know there's no returning;
　Once you go out, it's done, it's done.
All of my days are gray with yearning.
　(Nevertheless, a girl needs fun.)

Little white love, perplexed and weary,
　Sadly your banner fluttered down.
Sullen the days, and dreary, dreary.
　(Which of the boys is still in town?)
Radiant and sure, you came a-flying;
　Puzzled, you left on lagging feet.
Slow in my breast, my heart is dying.
　(Nevertheless, a girl must eat.)

Little white love, I hailed you gladly;
　Now I must wave you out of sight.
Ah, but you used me badly, badly.
　(Who'd like to take me out tonight?)
All of the blundering words I've spoken,
　Little white love, forgive, forgive.
Once you went out, my heart fell, broken.
　(Nevertheless, a girl must live.)

COMMENT

Oh, life is a glorious cycle of song,
A medley of extemporanea;
And love is a thing that can never go wrong;
And I am Marie of Roumania.

PLEA

Secrets, you said, would hold us two apart;
  You'd have me know of you your least transgression,
And so the intimate places of your heart,
  Kneeling, you bared to me, as in confession.
Softly you told of loves that went before—
  Of clinging arms, of kisses gladly given;
Luxuriously clean of heart once more,
  You rose up, then, and stood before me, shriven.

When this, my day of happiness, is through,
  And love, that bloomed so fair, turns brown and brittle,
There is a thing that I shall ask of you—
  I, who have given so much, and asked so little.
Some day, when there's another in my stead,
  Again you'll feel the need of absolution,
And you will go to her, and bow your head,
  And offer her your past, as contribution.

When with your list of loves you overcome her,
For Heaven's sake, keep this one secret from her!

PATTERN

Leave me to my lonely pillow.
    Go, and take your silly posies;
Who has vowed to wear the willow
    Looks a fool, tricked out in roses.

Who are you, my lad, to ease me?
    Leave your pretty words unspoken.
Tinkling echoes little please me,
    Now my heart is freshly broken.

Over young are you to guide me,
    And your blood is slow and sleeping.
If you must, then sit beside me. . . .
    Tell me, why have I been weeping?

DE PROFUNDIS

Oh, is it, then, Utopian
To hope that I may meet a man
Who'll not relate, in accents suave,
The tales of girls he used to have?

THEY PART

And if, my friend, you'd have it end,
   There's naught to hear or tell.
But need you try to black my eye
   In wishing me farewell?

Though I admit an edgèd wit
   In woe is warranted,
May I be frank? . . . Such words as "‗
   Are better left unsaid.

There's rosemary for you and me;
   But is it usual, dear,
To hire a man, and fill a van
   By way of *souvenir?*

BALLADE OF A GREAT WEARINESS

There's little to have but the things I had,
  There's little to bear but the things I bore.
There's nothing to carry and naught to add,
  And glory to Heaven, I paid the score.
There's little to do but I did before,
  There's little to learn but the things I know;
And this is the sum of a lasting lore:
  Scratch a lover, and find a foe.

And couldn't it be I was young and mad
  If ever my heart on my sleeve I wore?
There's many to claw at a heart unclad,
  And little the wonder it ripped and tore.
There's one that'll join in their push and roar,
  With stories to jabber, and stones to throw;
He'll fetch you a lesson that costs you sore—
  Scratch a lover, and find a foe.

So little I'll offer to you, my lad;
  It's little in loving I set my store.
There's many a maid would be flushed and glad,
  And better you'll knock at a kindlier door.
I'll dig at my lettuce, and sweep my floor—
  Forever, forever I'm done with woe—
And happen I'll whistle about my chore,
  "Scratch a lover, and find a foe."

L'ENVOI

Oh, beggar or prince, no more, no more!
   Be off and away with your strut and show.
The sweeter the apple, the blacker the core—
   Scratch a lover, and find a foe!

RÉSUMÉ

Razors pain you;
Rivers are damp;
Acids stain you;
And drugs cause cramp.
Guns aren't lawful;
Nooses give;
Gas smells awful;
You might as well live.

RENUNCIATION

Chloe's hair, no doubt, was brighter;
   Lydia's mouth more sweetly sad;
Hebe's arms were rather whiter;
   Languorous-lidded Helen had
Eyes more blue than e'er the sky was;
   Lalage's was subtler stuff;
Still, you used to think that I was
   Fair enough.

Now you're casting yearning glances
   At the pale Penelope;
Cutting in on Claudia's dances;
   Taking Iris out to tea.
Iole you find warm-hearted;
   Zoe's cheek is far from rough—
Don't you think it's time we parted? .
   Fair enough!

THE VETERAN

When I was young and bold and strong,
Oh, right was right, and wrong was wrong!
My plume on high, my flag unfurled,
I rode away to right the world.
"Come out, you dogs, and fight!" said I,
And wept there was but once to die.

But I am old; and good and bad
Are woven in a crazy plaid.
I sit and say, "The world is so;
And he is wise who lets it go.
A battle lost, a battle won—
The difference is small, my son."

Inertia rides and riddles me;
The which is called Philosophy.

PROPHETIC SOUL

Because your eyes are slant and slow,
  Because your hair is sweet to touch,
My heart is high again; but oh,
  I doubt if this will get me much.

VERSE FOR A CERTAIN DOG

Such glorious faith as fills your limpid eyes,
   Dear little friend of mine, I never knew.
All-innocent are you, and yet all-wise.
   (For Heaven's sake, stop worrying that shoe!)
You look about, and all you see is fair;
   This mighty globe was made for you alone.
Of all the thunderous ages, you're the heir.
   (Get off the pillow with that dirty bone!)

A skeptic world you face with steady gaze;
   High in young pride you hold your noble head;
Gayly you meet the rush of roaring days.
   (Must you eat puppy biscuit on the bed?)
Lancelike your courage, gleaming swift and strong,
   Yours the white rapture of a wingèd soul,
Yours is a spirit like a May-day song.
   (God help you, if you break the goldfish bowl!)

"Whatever is, is good"—your gracious creed.
   You wear your joy of living like a crown.
Love lights your simplest act, your every deed.
   (Drop it, I tell you—put that kitten down!)
You are God's kindliest gift of all—a friend.
   Your shining loyalty unflecked by doubt,
You ask but leave to follow to the end.
   (Couldn't you wait until I took you out?)

GODSPEED

Oh, seek, my love, your newer way;
  I'll not be left in sorrow.
So long as I have yesterday,
  Go take your damned tomorrow!

SONG OF PERFECT PROPRIETY

Oh, I should like to ride the seas,
   A roaring buccaneer;
A cutlass banging at my knees,
   A dirk behind my ear.
And when my captives' chains would clank
   I'd howl with glee and drink,
And then fling out the quivering plank
   And watch the beggars sink.

I'd like to straddle gory decks,
   And dig in laden sands,
And know the feel of throbbing necks
   Between my knotted hands.
Oh, I should like to strut and curse
   Among my blackguard crew. . . .
But I am writing little verse,
   As little ladies do.

Oh, I should like to dance and laugh
   And pose and preen and sway,
And rip the hearts of men in half,
   And toss the bits away.
I'd like to view the reeling years
   Through unastonished eyes,
And dip my finger-tips in tears,
   And give my smiles for sighs.

I'd stroll beyond the ancient bounds,
   And tap at fastened gates,
And hear the prettiest of sounds—
   The clink of shattered fates.
My slaves I'd like to bind with thongs
   That cut and burn and chill. . . .
But I am writing little songs,
   As little ladies will.

SOCIAL NOTE

Lady, lady, should you meet
One whose ways are all discreet,
One who murmurs that his wife
Is the lodestar of his life,
One who keeps assuring you
That he never was untrue,
Never loved another one . . .
Lady, lady, better run!

ONE PERFECT ROSE

A single flow'r he sent me, since we met.
    All tenderly his messenger he chose;
Deep-hearted, pure, with scented dew still wet—
    One perfect rose.

I knew the language of the floweret;
    "My fragile leaves," it said, "his heart enclose."
Love long has taken for his amulet
    One perfect rose.

Why is it no one ever sent me yet
    One perfect limousine, do you suppose?
Ah no, it's always just my luck to get
    One perfect rose.

BALLADE AT THIRTY-FIVE

This, no song of an ingénue,
    This, no ballad of innocence;
This, the rhyme of a lady who
    Followed ever her natural bents.
    This, a solo of sapience,
This, a chantey of sophistry,
    This, the sum of experiments—
I loved them until they loved me.

Decked in garments of sable hue,
    Daubed with ashes of myriad Lents,
Wearing shower bouquets of rue,
    Walk I ever in penitence.
    Oft I roam, as my heart repents,
Through God's acre of memory,
    Marking stones, in my reverence,
"I loved them until they loved me."

Pictures pass me in long review—
    Marching columns of dead events.
I was tender and, often, true;
    Ever a prey to coincidence.
    Always knew I the consequence;
Always saw what the end would be.
    We're as Nature has made us—hence
I loved them until they loved me.

L'ENVOI

Princes, never I'd give offense,
    Won't you think of me tenderly?   -
Here's my strength and my weakness, gents-
    I loved them until they loved me.

THE THIN EDGE

With you, my heart is quiet here,
And all my thoughts are cool as rain.
I sit and let the shifting year
Go by before the windowpane,
And reach my hand to yours, my dear
I wonder what it's like in Spain.

LOVE SONG

My own dear love, he is strong and bold
  And he cares not what comes after.
His words ring sweet as a chime of gold,
  And his eyes are lit with laughter.
He is jubilant as a flag unfurled—
  Oh, a girl, she'd not forget him.
My own dear love, he is all my world—
  And I wish I'd never met him.

My love, he's mad, and my love, he's fleet,
  And a wild young wood-thing bore him!
The ways are fair to his roaming feet,
  And the skies are sunlit for him.
As sharply sweet to my heart he seems
  As the fragrance of acacia.
My own dear love, he is all my dreams—
  And I wish he were in Asia.

My love runs by like a day in June,
  And he makes no friends of sorrows.
He'll tread his galloping rigadoon
  In the pathway of the morrows.
He'll live his days where the sunbeams start,
  Nor could storm or wind uproot him.
My own dear love, he is all my heart—
  And I wish somebody'd shoot him.

INDIAN SUMMER

In youth, it was a way I had
   To do my best to please,
And change, with every passing lad,
   To suit his theories.

But now I know the things I know,
   And do the things I do;
And if you do not like me so,
   To hell, my love, with you!

PHILOSOPHY

If I should labor through daylight and dark,
   Consecrate, valorous, serious, true,
Then on the world I may blazon my mark;
   And what if I don't, and what if I do?

FOR AN UNKNOWN LADY

Lady, if you'd slumber sound,
Keep your eyes upon the ground.
If you'd toss and turn at night,
Slip your glances left and right.
Would the mornings find you gay,
Never give your heart away.
Would they find you pale and sad,
Fling it to a whistling lad.
Ah, but when his pleadings burn,
Will you let my words return?
Will you lock your pretty lips,
And deny your finger-tips,
Veil away your tender eyes,
Just because some words were wise?
If he whistles low and clear
When the insistent moon is near
And the secret stars are known—
Will your heart be still your own
Just because some words were true? .
Lady, I was told them, too!

THE LEAL

The friends I made have slipped and strayed.
  And who's the one that cares?
A trifling lot and best forgot—
  And that's my tale, and theirs.

Then if my friendships break and bend,
  There's little need to cry
The while I know that every foe
  Is faithful till I die.

WORDS OF COMFORT TO BE
SCRATCHED ON A MIRROR

Helen of Troy had a wandering glance;
Sappho's restriction was only the sky;
Ninon was ever the chatter of France;
But oh, what a good girl am I!

MEN

They hail you as their morning star
Because you are the way you are.
If you return the sentiment,
They'll try to make you different;
And once they have you, safe and sound,
They want to change you all around.
Your moods and ways they put a curse on;
They'd make of you another person.
They cannot let you go your gait;
They influence and educate.
They'd alter all that they admired.
They make me sick, they make me tired.

NEWS ITEM

Men seldom make passes
At girls who wear glasses.

SONG OF ONE OF THE GIRLS

Here in my heart I am Helen;
  I'm Aspasia and Hero, at least.
I'm Judith, and Jael, and Madame de Staël;
  I'm Salome, moon of the East.

Here in my soul I am Sappho;
  Lady Hamilton am I, as well.
In me Récamier vies with Kitty O'Shea,
  With Dido, and Eve, and poor Nell.

I'm of the glamorous ladies
  At whose beckoning history shook.
But you are a man, and see only my pan,
  So I stay at home with a book.

LULLABY

Sleep, pretty lady, the night is enfolding you;
   Drift, and so lightly, on crystalline streams.
Wrapped in its perfumes, the darkness is holding you;
   Starlight bespangles the way of your dreams.
Chorus the nightingales, wistfully amorous;
   Blessedly quiet, the blare of the day.
All the sweet hours may your visions be glamorous—
   Sleep, pretty lady, as long as you may.

Sleep, pretty lady, the night shall be still for you;
   Silvered and silent, it watches your rest.
Each little breeze, in its eagerness, will for you
   Murmur the melodies ancient and blest.
So in the midnight does happiness capture us;
   Morning is dim with another day's tears.
Give yourself sweetly to images rapturous—
   Sleep, pretty lady, a couple of years.

Sleep, pretty lady, the world awaits day with you;
   Girlish and golden, the slender young moon.
Grant the fond darkness its mystical way with you;
   Morning returns to us ever too soon.
Roses unfold, in their loveliness, all for you;
   Blossom the lilies for hope of your glance.
When you're awake, all the men go and fall for you—
   Sleep, pretty lady, and give me a chance.

FAUTE DE MIEUX

Travel, trouble, music, art,
    A kiss, a frock, a rhyme—
I never said they feed my heart,
    But still they pass my time.

ROUNDEL

She's passing fair; but so demure is she,
So quiet is her gown, so smooth her hair,
That few there are who note her and agree
  She's passing fair.

Yet when was ever beauty held more rare
Than simple heart and maiden modesty?
What fostered charms with virtue could compare?

Alas, no lover ever stops to see;
The best that she is offered is the air.
Yet—if the passing mark is minus D—
  She's passing fair.

A CERTAIN LADY

Oh, I can smile for you, and tilt my head,
  And drink your rushing words with eager lips,
And paint my mouth for you a fragrant red,
  And trace your brows with tutored finger-tips.
When you rehearse your list of loves to me,
  Oh, I can laugh and marvel, rapturous-eyed.
And you laugh back, nor can you ever see
  The thousand little deaths my heart has died.
And you believe, so well I know my part,
  That I am gay as morning, light as snow,
And all the straining things within my heart
  You'll never know.

Oh, I can laugh and listen, when we meet,
  And you bring tales of fresh adventurings—
Of ladies delicately indiscreet,
  Of lingering hands, and gently whispered things.
And you are pleased with me, and strive anew
  To sing me sagas of your late delights.
Thus do you want me—marveling, gay, and true—
  Nor do you see my staring eyes of nights.
And when, in search of novelty, you stray,
  Oh, I can kiss you blithely as you go. . . .
And what goes on, my love, while you're away,
  You'll never know.

OBSERVATION

If I don't drive around the park,
I'm pretty sure to make my mark.
If I'm in bed each night by ten,
I may get back my looks again.
If I abstain from fun and such,
I'll probably amount to much;
But I shall stay the way I am,
Because I do not give a damn.

SYMPTOM RECITAL

I do not like my state of mind;
I'm bitter, querulous, unkind.
I hate my legs, I hate my hands,
I do not yearn for lovelier lands.
I dread the dawn's recurrent light;
I hate to go to bed at night.
I snoot at simple, earnest folk.
I cannot take the gentlest joke.
I find no peace in paint or type.
My world is but a lot of tripe.
I'm disillusioned, empty-breasted.
For what I think, I'd be arrested.
I am not sick, I am not well.
My quondam dreams are shot to hell.
My soul is crushed, my spirit sore;
I do not like me any more.
I cavil, quarrel, grumble, grouse.
I ponder on the narrow house.
I shudder at the thought of men. . .
I'm due to fall in love again.

RONDEAU REDOUBLE

(AND SCARCELY WORTH THE TROUBLE, AT THAT)

The same to me are somber days and gay.
  Though joyous dawns the rosy morn, and bright,
Because my dearest love is gone away
  Within my heart is melancholy night.

My heart beats low in loneliness, despite
  That riotous Summer holds the earth in sway.
In cerements my spirit is bedight;
  The same to me are somber days and gay.

Though breezes in the rippling grasses play,
  And waves dash high and far in glorious might,
I thrill no longer to the sparkling day,
  Though joyous dawns the rosy morn, and bright.

Ungraceful seems to me the swallow's flight;
  As well might heaven's blue be sullen gray;
My soul discerns no beauty in their sight
  Because my dearest love is gone away.

Let roses fling afar their crimson spray,
  And virgin daisies splash the fields with white,
Let bloom the poppy hotly as it may,
  Within my heart is melancholy night.

And this, O love, my pitiable plight
   Whenever from my circling arms you stray;
This little world of mine has lost its light. . . .
   I hope to God, my dear, that you can say
                              The same to me.

FIGHTING WORDS

Say my love is easy had,
   Say I'm bitten raw with pride,
Say I am too often sad—
   Still behold me at your side.

Say I'm neither brave nor young,
   Say I woo and coddle care,
Say the devil touched my tongue—
   Still you have my heart to wear.

But say my verses do not scan,
   And I get me another man!

THE CHOICE

He'd have given me rolling lands,
  Houses of marble, and billowing farms,
Pearls, to trickle between my hands,
  Smoldering rubies, to circle my arms.
You—you'd only a lilting song,
  Only a melody, happy and high,
You were sudden and swift and strong—
  Never a thought for another had I.

He'd have given me laces rare,
  Dresses that glimmered with frosty sheen,
Shining ribbons to wrap my hair,
  Horses to draw me, as fine as a queen.
You—you'd only to whistle low,
  Gayly I followed wherever you led.
I took you, and I let him go—
  Somebody ought to examine my head!

GENERAL REVIEW OF THE
SEX SITUATION

Woman wants monogamy;
Man delights in novelty.
Love is woman's moon and sun;
Man has other forms of fun.
Woman lives but in her lord;
Count to ten, and man is bored.
With this the gist and sum of it,
What earthly good can come of it?

INSCRIPTION FOR THE CEILING
OF A BEDROOM

Daily dawns another day;
I must up, to make my way.
Though I dress and drink and eat,
Move my fingers and my feet,
Learn a little, here and there,
Weep and laugh and sweat and swear,
Hear a song, or watch a stage,
Leave some words upon a page,
Claim a foe, or hail a friend—
Bed awaits me at the end.

Though I go in pride and strength,
I'll come back to bed at length.
Though I walk in blinded woe,
Back to bed I'm bound to go.
High my heart, or bowed my head,
All my days but lead to bed.
Up, and out, and on; and then
Ever back to bed again,
Summer, Winter, Spring, and Fall—
I'm a fool to rise at all!

PICTURES IN THE SMOKE .

Oh, gallant was the first love, and glittering and fine;
The second love was water, in a clear white cup;
The third love was his, and the fourth was mine;
And after that, I always get them all mixed up.

NOCTURNE

Always I knew that it could not last
   (Gathering clouds, and the snowflakes flying),
Now it is part of the golden past
   (Darkening skies, and the night-wind sighing),
It is but cowardice to pretend.
   Cover with ashes our love's cold crater—
Always I've known that it had to end
   Sooner or later.

Always I knew it would come like this
   (Pattering rain, and the grasses springing),
Sweeter to you is a new love's kiss
   (Flickering sunshine, and young birds singing).
Gone are the raptures that once we knew,
   Now you are finding a new joy greater—
Well, I'll be doing the same thing, too,
   Sooner or later.

INTERVIEW

The ladies men admire, I've heard,
Would shudder at a wicked word.
Their candle gives a single light;
They'd rather stay at home at night.
They do not keep awake till three,
Nor read erotic poetry.
They never sanction the impure,
Nor recognize an overture.
They shrink from powders and from paints
So far, I've had no complaints.

EXPERIENCE

Some men break your heart in two,
    Some men fawn and flatter,
Some men never look at you;
    And that cleans up the matter.

NEITHER BLOODY NOR BOWED

They say of me, and so they should,
It's doubtful if I come to good.
I see acquaintances and friends
Accumulating dividends,
And making enviable names
In science, art, and parlor games.
But I, despite expert advice,
Keep doing things I think are nice,
And though to good I never come—
Inseparable my nose and thumb!

THE BURNED CHILD

Love has had his way with me.
  This my heart is torn and maimed
Since he took his play with me.
  Cruel well the bow-boy aimed,

Shot, and saw the feathered shaft
  Dripping bright and bitter red.
He that shrugged his wings and laughed-
  Better had he left me dead.

Sweet, why do you plead me, then,
  Who have bled so sore of that?
Could I bear it once again? . . .
  Drop a hat, dear, drop a hat!

SUNSET
GUN

GODMOTHER

The day that I was christened—
    It's a hundred years, and more!—
A hag came and listened
    At the white church door,
A-hearing her that bore me
    And all my kith and kin
Considerately, for me,
    Renouncing sin.
While some gave me corals,
    And some gave me gold,
And porringers, with morals
    Agreeably scrolled,
The hag stood, buckled
    In a dim gray cloak;
Stood there and chuckled,
    Spat, and spoke:
"There's few enough in life'll
    Be needing my help,
But I've got a trifle
    For your fine young whelp.
I give her sadness,
    And the gift of pain,
The new-moon madness,
    And the love of rain."
And little good to leave me
    In their holy silver bowl
After what she gave me—
    Rest her soul!

PARTIAL COMFORT

Whose love is given over-well
Shall look on Helen's face in hell,
Whilst they whose love is thin and wise
May view John Knox in paradise.

THE RED DRESS

I always saw, I always said
   If I were grown and free,
I'd have a gown of reddest red
   As fine as you could see,

To wear out walking, sleek and slow,
   Upon a Summer day,
And there'd be one to see me so,
   And flip the world away.

And he would be a gallant one,
   With stars behind his eyes,
And hair like metal in the sun,
   And lips too warm for lies.

I always saw us, gay and good,
   High honored in the town.
Now I am grown to womanhood. . .
   I have the silly gown.

VICTORIA

Dear dead Victoria
  Rotted cosily;
In excelsis gloria,
  And R. I. P.

And her shroud was buttoned neat,
  And her bones were clean and round,
And her soul was at her feet
  Like a bishop's marble hound.

Albert lay a-drying,
  Lavishly arrayed,
With his soul out flying
  Where his heart had stayed.

And there's some could tell you what land
  His spirit walks serene
(But I've heard them say in Scotland
  It's never been seen).

THE COUNSELOR

I met a man the other day—
   A kindly man, and serious—
Who viewed me in a thoughtful way,
   And spoke me so, and spoke me thus:

"Oh, dallying's a sad mistake;
   'Tis craven to survey the morrow!
Go give your heart, and if it break—
   A wise companion is Sorrow.

"Oh, live, my child, nor keep your soul
   To crowd your coffin when you're dead. . . .'
I asked his work; he dealt in coal,
   And shipped it up the Tyne, he said.

PARABLE FOR A CERTAIN VIRGIN

Oh, ponder, friend, the porcupine;
   Refresh your recollection,
And sit a moment, to define
   His means of self-protection.

How truly fortified is he!
   Where is the beast his double
In forethought of emergency
   And readiness for trouble?

Recall his figure, and his shade—
   How deftly planned and clearly
For slithering through the dappled glade
   Unseen, or pretty nearly.

Yet should an alien eye discern
   His presence in the woodland,
How little has he left to learn
   Of self-defense! My good land!

For he can run, as swift as sound,
   To where his goose may hang high;
Or thrust his head against the ground
   And tunnel half to Shanghai;

Or he can climb the dizziest bough—
   Unhesitant, mechanic—
And, resting, dash from off his brow
   The bitter beads of panic;

Or should pursuers press him hot,
    One scarcely needs to mention
His quick and cruel barbs, that got
    Shakespearean attention;

Or driven to his final ditch,
    To his extremest thicket,
He'll fight with claws and molars (which
    Is not considered cricket).

How amply armored, he, to fend
    The fear of chase that haunts him!
How well prepared our little friend!—
    And who the devil wants him?

BRIC-A-BRAC

Little things that no one needs—
   Little things to joke about—
Little landscapes, done in beads.
   Little morals, woven out,
Little wreaths of gilded grass,
   Little brigs of whittled oak
Bottled painfully in glass;
   These are made by lonely folk.

Lonely folk have lines of days
   Long and faltering and thin;
Therefore—little wax bouquets,
   Prayers cut upon a pin,
Little maps of pinkish lands,
   Little charts of curly seas,
Little plats of linen strands,
   Little verses, such as these.

INTERIOR

Her mind lives in a quiet room,
   A narrow room, and tall,
With pretty lamps to quench the gloom
   And mottoes on the wall.

There all the things are waxen neat
   And set in decorous lines;
And there are posies, round and sweet,
   And little, straightened vines.

Her mind lives tidily, apart
   From cold and noise and pain,
And bolts the door against her heart,
   Out wailing in the rain.

REUBEN'S CHILDREN

Accursed from their birth they be
Who seek to find monogamy,
Pursuing it from bed to bed—
I think they would be better dead.

ON CHEATING THE FIDDLER

"Then we will have tonight!" we said.
"Tomorrow—may we not be dead?"
The morrow touched our eyes, and found
Us walking firm above the ground,
Our pulses quick, our blood alight.
Tomorrow's gone—we'll have tonight!

THERE WAS ONE

There was one a-riding grand
    On a tall brown mare,
And a fine gold band
    He brought me there.

A little, gold band
    He held to me
That would shine on a hand
    For the world to see.

There was one a-walking swift
    To a little, new song,
And a rose was the gift
    He carried along,

First of all the posies,
    Dewy and red.
They that have roses
    Never need bread.

There was one with a swagger
    And a soft, slow tongue,
And a bright, cold dagger
    Where his left hand swung—

Carven and gilt,
    Old and bad—
And his stroking of the hilt
    Set a girl mad.

There was one a-riding grand
    As he rode from me.
And he raised his golden band
    And he threw it in the sea.

There was one a-walking slow
    To a sad, long sigh.
And his rose drooped low,
    And he flung it down to die.

There was one with a swagger
    And a little, sharp pride,
And a bright, cold dagger
    Ever at his side.

At his side it stayed
    When he ran to part.
What is this blade
    Struck through my heart?

INCURABLE

And if my heart be scarred and burned,
The safer, I, for all I learned;
The calmer, I, to see it true
That ways of love are never new—
The love that sets you daft and dazed
Is every love that ever blazed;
The happier, I, to fathom this:
A kiss is every other kiss.
The reckless vow, the lovely name,
When Helen walked, were spoke the same;
The weighted breast, the grinding woe,
When Phaon fled, were ever so.
Oh, it is sure as it is sad
That any lad is every lad,
And what's a girl, to dare implore
Her dear be hers forevermore?
Though he be tried and he be bold,
And swearing death should he be cold,
He'll run the path the others went. . . .
But you, my sweet, are different.

FABLE

Oh, there once was a lady, and so I've been told,
Whose lover grew weary, whose lover grew cold.
"My child," he remarked, "though our episode ends,
In the manner of men, I suggest we be friends."
And the truest of friends ever after they were—
Oh, they lied in their teeth when they told me of her!

THE SECOND OLDEST STORY

Go I must along my ways
  Though my heart be ragged,
Dripping bitter through the days,
  Festering, and jagged.
Smile I must at every twinge,
  Kiss, to time its throbbing;
He that tears a heart to fringe
  Hates the noise of sobbing.

Weep, my love, till Heaven hears;
  Curse and moan and languish.
While I wash your wound with tears,
  Ease aloud your anguish.
Bellow of the pit in Hell
  Where you're made to linger.
There and there and well and well—
  Did he prick his finger!

A PIG'S-EYE VIEW OF LITERATURE

THE LIVES AND TIMES OF JOHN KEATS,
PERCY BYSSHE SHELLEY, AND
GEORGE GORDON NOEL, LORD BYRON

Byron and Shelley and Keats
Were a trio of lyrical treats.
The forehead of Shelley was cluttered with curls,
And Keats never was a descendant of earls,
And Byron walked out with a number of girls,
But it didn't impair the poetical feats
Of Byron and Shelley,
Of Byron and Shelley,
Of Byron and Shelley and Keats.

OSCAR WILDE

If, with the literate, I am
Impelled to try an epigram,
I never seek to take the credit;
We all assume that Oscar said it.

HARRIET BEECHER STOWE

The pure and worthy Mrs. Stowe
Is one we all are proud to know
As mother, wife, and authoress—
Thank God, I am content with less!

D. G. ROSSETTI

Dante Gabriel Rossetti
Buried all of his *libretti*,
Thought the matter over—then
Went and dug them up again.

THOMAS CARLYLE

Carlyle combined the lit'ry life
With throwing teacups at his wife,
Remarking, rather testily,
"Oh, stop your dodging, Mrs. C.!"

CHARLES DICKENS

Who call him spurious and shoddy
Shall do it o'er my lifeless body.
I heartily invite such birds
To come outside and say those words!

ALEXANDRE DUMAS AND HIS SON

Although I work, and seldom cease.
At Dumas *père* and Dumas *fils*,
Alas, I cannot make me care
For Dumas *fils* and Dumas *père*.

ALFRED, LORD TENNYSON

Should Heaven send me any son,
I hope he's not like Tennyson.
I'd rather have him play a fiddle
Than rise and bow and speak an idyll.

GEORGE GISSING

When I admit neglect of Gissing,
They say I don't know what I'm missing.
Until their arguments are subtler,
I think I'll stick to Samuel Butler.

WALTER SAVAGE LANDOR

Upon the work of Walter Landor
I am unfit to write with candor.
If you can read it, well and good;
But as for me, I never could.

GEORGE SAND

What time the gifted lady took
Away from paper, pen, and book,
She spent in amorous dalliance
(They do those things so well in France).

MORTAL ENEMY ·

Let another cross his way—
   She's the one will do the weeping!
Little need I fear he'll stray
   Since I have his heart in keeping.

Let another hail him dear—
   Little chance that he'll forget me!
Only need I curse and fear
   Her he loved before he met me.

PENELOPE

In the pathway of the sun,
   In the footsteps of the breeze,
Where the world and sky are one,
   He shall ride the silver seas,
      He shall cut the glittering wave.
I shall sit at home, and rock;
Rise, to heed a neighbor's knock;
Brew my tea, and snip my thread;
Bleach the linen for my bed.
      They will call him brave.

BOHEMIA

Authors and actors and artists and such
Never know nothing, and never know much.
Sculptors and singers and those of their kidney
Tell their affairs from Seattle to Sydney.
Playwrights and poets and such horses' necks
Start off from anywhere, end up at sex.
Diarists, critics, and similar roe
Never say nothing, and never say no.
People Who Do Things exceed my endurance;
God, for a man that solicits insurance!

THE SEARCHED SOUL

When I consider, pro and con,
What things my love is built upon—
A curly mouth; a sinewed wrist;
A questioning brow; a pretty twist
Of words as old and tried as sin;
A pointed ear; a cloven chin;
Long, tapered limbs; and slanted eyes
Not cold nor kind nor darkly wise—
When so I ponder, here apart,
What shallow boons suffice my heart,
What dust-bound trivia capture me,
I marvel at my normalcy.

THE TRUSTING HEART

Oh, I'd been better dying,
   Oh, I was slow and sad;
A fool I was, a-crying
   About a cruel lad!

But there was one that found me,
   That wept to see me weep,
And had his arm around me,
   And gave me words to keep.

And I'd be better dying,
   And I am slow and sad;
A fool I am, a-crying
   About a tender lad!

THOUGHT FOR A SUNSHINY MORNING

It costs me never a stab nor squirm
To tread by chance upon a worm.
"Aha, my little dear," I say,
"Your clan will pay me back one day."

THE GENTLEST LADY

They say He was a serious child,
  And quiet in His ways;
They say the gentlest lady smiled
  To hear the neighbors' praise.

The coffers of her heart would close
  Upon their smallest word.
Yet did they say, "How tall He grows!"
  They thought she had not heard.

They say upon His birthday eve
  She'd rock Him to His rest
As if she could not have Him leave
  The shelter of her breast.

The poor must go in bitter thrift,
  The poor must give in pain,
But ever did she set a gift
  To greet His day again.

They say she'd kiss the Boy awake,
  And hail Him gay and clear,
But oh, her heart was like to break
  To count another year.

THE MAID-SERVANT AT THE INN

"It's queer," she said; "I see the light
    As plain as I beheld it then,
All silver-like and calm and bright—
    We've not had stars like that again!

"And she was such a gentle thing
    To birth a baby in the cold.
The barn was dark and frightening—
    This new one's better than the old.

"I mind my eyes were full of tears,
    For I was young, and quick distressed,
But she was less than me in years
    That held a son against her breast.

"I never saw a sweeter child—
    The little one, the darling one!—
I mind I told her, when he smiled
    You'd know he was his mother's son.

"It's queer that I should see them so—
    The time they came to Bethlehem
Was more than thirty years ago;
    I've prayed that all is well with them."

FULFILLMENT

For this my mother wrapped me warm,
And called me home against the storm,
And coaxed my infant nights to quiet,
And gave me roughage in my diet,
And tucked me in my bed at eight,
And clipped my hair, and marked my weight,
And watched me as I sat and stood:
That I might grow to womanhood
To hear a whistle and drop my wits
And break my heart to clattering bits.

DAYLIGHT SAVING

My answers are inadequate
To those demanding day and date,
And ever set a tiny shock
Through strangers asking what's o'clock;
Whose days are spent in whittling rhyme-
What's time to her, or she to Time?

SURPRISE

My heart went fluttering with fear
Lest you should go, and leave me here
To beat my breast and rock my head
And stretch me sleepless on my bed.
Ah, clear they see and true they say
That one shall weep, and one shall stray
For such is Love's unvarying law. . . .
I never thought, I never saw
That I should be the first to go;
How pleasant that it happened so!

ON BEING A WOMAN

Why is it, when I am in Rome,
I'd give an eye to be at home,
But when on native earth I be,
My soul is sick for Italy?

And why with you, my love, my lord,
Am I spectacularly bored,
Yet do you up and leave me—then
I scream to have you back again?

AFTERNOON

When I am old, and comforted,
  And done with this desire,
With Memory to share my bed
  And Peace to share my fire,

I'll comb my hair in scalloped bands
  Beneath my laundered cap,
And watch my cool and fragile hands
  Lie light upon my lap.

And I will have a spriggèd gown
  With lace to kiss my throat;
I'll draw my curtain to the town,
  And hum a purring note.

And I'll forget the way of tears,
  And rock, and stir my tea.
But oh, I wish those blessed years
  Were further than they be!

A DREAM LIES DEAD

A dream lies dead here. May you softly go
Before this place, and turn away your eyes,
Nor seek to know the look of that which dies
Importuning Life for life. Walk not in woe,
But, for a little, let your step be slow.
And, of your mercy, be not sweetly wise
With words of hope and Spring and tenderer
A dream lies dead; and this all mourners know:

Whenever one drifted petal leaves the tree—
Though white of bloom as it had been before
And proudly waitful of fecundity—
One little loveliness can be no more;
And so must Beauty bow her imperfect head
Because a dream has joined the wistful dead!

THE HOMEBODY

There still are kindly things for me to know,
Who am afraid to dream, afraid to feel—
This little chair of scrubbed and sturdy deal,
This easy book, this fire, sedate and slow.
And I shall stay with them, nor cry the woe
Of wounds across my breast that do not heal;
Nor wish that Beauty drew a duller steel,
Since I am sworn to meet her as a foe.

It may be, when the devil's own time is done,
That I shall hear the dropping of the rain
At midnight, and lie quiet in my bed;
Or stretch and straighten to the yellow sun;
Or face the turning tree, and have no pain;
So shall I learn at last my heart is dead.

SECOND LOVE

"So surely is she mine," you say, and turn
Your quick and steady mind to harder things—
To bills and bonds and talk of what men earn—
And whistle up the stair, of evenings.
And do you see a dream behind my eyes,
Or ask a simple question twice of me—
"Thus women are," you say; for men are wise
And tolerant, in their security.

How shall I count the midnights I have known
When calm you turn to me, nor feel me start,
To find my easy lips upon your own
And know my breast beneath your rhythmic heart.
Your god defer the day I tell you this:
My lad, my lad, it is not you I kiss!

FAIR WEATHER

This level reach of blue is not my sea;
Here are sweet waters, pretty in the sun,
Whose quiet ripples meet obediently
A marked and measured line, one after one.
This is no sea of mine, that humbly laves
Untroubled sands, spread glittering and warm.
I have a need of wilder, crueler waves;
They sicken of the calm, who knew the storm.

So let a love beat over me again,
Loosing its million desperate breakers wide;
Sudden and terrible to rise and wane;
Roaring the heavens apart; a reckless tide
That casts upon the heart, as it recedes,
Splinters and spars and dripping, salty weeds.

THE WHISTLING GIRL

Back of my back, they talk of me,
  Gabble and honk and hiss;
Let them batten, and let them be—
  Me, I can sing them this:

"Better to shiver beneath the stars,
  Head on a faithless breast,
Than peer at the night through rusted bars,
  And share an irksome rest.

"Better to see the dawn come up,
  Along of a trifling one,
Than set a steady man's cloth and cup
  And pray the day be done.

"Better be left by twenty dears
  Than lie in a loveless bed;
Better a loaf that's wet with tears
  Than cold, unsalted bread."

Back of my back, they wag their chins,
  Whinny and bleat and sigh;
But better a heart a-bloom with sins
  Than hearts gone yellow and dry!

STORY

"And if he's gone away," said she,
"Good riddance, if you're asking me.
I'm not a one to lie awake
And weep for anybody's sake.
There's better lads than him about!
I'll wear my buckled slippers out
A-dancing till the break of day.
I'm better off with him away!
And if he never come," said she,
"Now what on earth is that to me?
I wouldn't have him back!"
                              I hope
Her mother washed her mouth with soap.

FRUSTRATION

If I had a shiny gun,
I could have a world of fun
Speeding bullets through the brains
Of the folk who give me pains;

Or had I some poison gas,
I could make the moments pass
Bumping off a number of
People whom I do not love.

But I have no lethal weapon—
Thus does Fate our pleasure step on!
So they still are quick and well
Who should be, by rights, in hell.

HEALED

Oh, when I flung my heart away,
  The year was at its fall.
I saw my dear, the other day,
  Beside a flowering wall;
And this was all I had to say:
  "I thought that he was tall!"

LANDSCAPE

Now this must be the sweetest place
    From here to heaven's end;
The field is white with flowering lace,
    The birches leap and bend,

The hills, beneath the roving sun,
    From green to purple pass,
And little, trifling breezes run
    Their fingers through the grass.

So good it is, so gay it is,
    So calm it is, and pure,
A one whose eyes may look on this
    Must be the happier, sure.

But me—I see it flat and gray
    And blurred with misery,
Because a lad a mile away
    Has little need of me.

POST-GRADUATE

Hope it was that tutored me,
    And Love that taught me more;
And now I learn at Sorrow's knee
    The self-same lore.

A FAVORITE GRANDDAUGHTER

Never love a simple lad,
   Guard against a wise,
Shun a timid youth and sad,
   Hide from haunted eyes.

Never hold your heart in pain
   For an evil-doer;
Never flip it down the lane
   To a gifted wooer.

Never love a loving son,
   Nor a sheep astray;
Gather up your skirts and run
   From a tender way.

Never give away a tear,
   Never toss and pine;
Should you heed my words, my dear,
   You're no blood of mine!

LIEBESTOD

When I was bold, when I was bold—
    And that's a hundred years!—
Oh, never I thought my breast could hold
    The terrible weight of tears.

I said: "Now some be dolorous;
    I hear them wail and sigh,
And if it be Love that play them thus,
    Then never a love will I."

I said: "I see them rack and rue,
    I see them wring and ache,
And little I'll crack my heart in two
    With little the heart can break."

When I was gay, when I was gay—
    It's ninety years and nine!—
Oh, never I thought that Death could lay
    His terrible hand in mine.

I said: "He plies his trade among
    The musty and infirm;
A body so hard and bright and young
    Could never be meat for worm."

"I see him dull their eyes," I said,
    "And still their rattling breath.
And how under God could I be dead
    That never was meant for Death?"

But Love came by, to quench my sleep,
  And here's my sundered heart;
And bitter's my woe, and black, and deep,
  And little I guessed a part.

Yet this there is to cool my breast,
  And this to ease my spell;
Now if I were Love's, like all the rest,
  Then can I be Death's, as well.

And he shall have me, sworn and bound,
  And I'll be done with Love.
And better I'll be below the ground
  Than ever I'll be above.

DILEMMA

If I were mild, and I were sweet,
And laid my heart before your feet,
And took my dearest thoughts to you,
And hailed your easy lies as true;
Were I to murmur "Yes," and then
"How true, my dear," and "Yes," again,
And wear my eyes discreetly down,
And tremble whitely at your frown,
And keep my words unquestioning—
My love, you'd run like anything!

Should I be frail, and I be mad,
And share my heart with every lad,
But beat my head against the floor
What times you wandered past my door;
Were I to doubt, and I to sneer,
And shriek "Farewell!" and still be here,
And break your joy, and quench your trust-
I should not see you for the dust!

THEORY

Into love and out again,
　　Thus I went, and thus I go.
Spare your voice, and hold your pen—
　　Well and bitterly I know
All the songs were ever sung,
　　All the words were ever said;
Could it be, when I was young,
　　Some one dropped me on my head?

A FAIRLY SAD TALE

I think that I shall never know
Why I am thus, and I am so.
Around me, other girls inspire
In men the rush and roar of fire,
The sweet transparency of glass,
The tenderness of April grass,
The durability of granite;
But me—I don't know how to plan it.
The lads I've met in Cupid's deadlock
Were—shall we say?—born out of wedlock.
They broke my heart, they stilled my song,
And said they had to run along,
Explaining, so to sop my tears,
First came their parents or careers.
But ever does experience
Deny me wisdom, calm, and sense!
Though she's a fool who seeks to capture
The twenty-first fine, careless rapture,
I must go on, till ends my rope,
Who from my birth was cursed with hope.
A heart in half is chaste, archaic;
But mine resembles a mosaic—
The thing's become ridiculous!
Why am I so? Why am I thus?

THE LAST QUESTION

New love, new love, where are you to lead me?
  All along a narrow way that marks a crooked line.
How are you to slake me, and how are you to feed me?
  With bitter yellow berries, and a sharp new wine.

New love, new love, shall I be forsaken?
  One shall go a-wandering, and one of us must sigh.
Sweet it is to slumber, but how shall we awaken—
  Whose will be the broken heart, when dawn comes by?

SUPERFLUOUS ADVICE

Should they whisper false of you,
   Never trouble to deny;
Should the words they say be true,
   Weep and storm and swear they lie.

BUT NOT FORGOTTEN

I think, no matter where you stray,
That I shall go with you a way.
Though you may wander sweeter lands,
You will not soon forget my hands,
Nor yet the way I held my head,
Nor all the tremulous things I said.
You still will see me, small and white
And smiling, in the secret night,
And feel my arms about you when
The day comes fluttering back again.
I think, no matter where you be,
You'll hold me in your memory
And keep my image, there without me,
By telling later loves about me.

TWO-VOLUME NOVEL

The sun's gone dim, and
   The moon's turned black;
For I loved him, and
   He didn't love back.

POUR PRENDRE CONGÉ

I'm sick of embarking in dories
   Upon an emotional sea.
I'm wearied of playing Dolores
   (A role never written for me).

I'll never again like a cub lick
   My wounds while I squeal at the hurt.
No more I'll go walking in public,
   My heart hanging out of my shirt.

I'm tired of entwining me garlands
   Of weather-worn hemlock and bay.
I'm over my longing for far lands—
   I wouldn't give that for Cathay.

I'm through with performing the ballet
   Of love unrequited and told.
Euterpe, I tender you *vale*;
   Good-by, and take care of that cold.

I'm done with this burning and giving
   And reeling the rhymes of my woes.
And how I'll be making my living,
   The Lord in His mystery knows.

A LADY WHO MUST WRITE VERSE

Unto seventy years and seven,
    Hide your double birthright well—
You, that are the brat of Heaven
    And the pampered heir to Hell.

Let your rhymes be tinsel treasures,
    Strung and seen and thrown aside.
Drill your apt and docile measures
    Sternly as you drill your pride.

Show your quick, alarming skill in
    Tidy mockeries of art;
Never, never dip your quill in
    Ink that rushes from your heart.

When your pain must come to paper,
    See it dust, before the day;
Let your night light curl and caper,
    Let it lick the words away.

Never print, poor child, a lay on
    Love and tears and anguishing,
Lest a cooled, benignant Phaon
    Murmur, "Silly little thing!"

RHYME AGAINST LIVING

If wild my breast and sore my pride,
I bask in dreams of suicide;
If cool my heart and high my head,
I think, "How lucky are the dead!"

WISDOM

This I say, and this I know:
   Love has seen the last of me.
Love's a trodden lane to woe,
   Love's a path to misery.

This I know, and knew before,
   This I tell you, of my years:
Hide your heart, and lock your door.
   Hell's afloat in lovers' tears.

Give your heart, and toss and moan;
   What a pretty fool you look!
I am sage, who sit alone;
   Here's my wool, and here's my book

Look! A lad's a-waiting there,
   Tall he is and bold, and gay.
What the devil do I care
   What I know, and what I say?

CODA

There's little in taking or giving,
    There's little in water or wine;
This living, this living, this living
    Was never a project of mine.
Oh, hard is the struggle, and sparse is
    The gain of the one at the top,
For art is a form of catharsis,
    And love is a permanent flop,
And work is the province of cattle,
    And rest's for a clam in a shell,
So I'm thinking of throwing the battle-
    Would you kindly direct me to hell?

DEATH
AND TAXES
AND
OTHER POEMS

PRAYER FOR A PRAYER

Dearest one, when I am dead
  Never seek to follow me.
    Never mount the quiet hill
    Where the copper leaves are still,
  As my heart is, on the tree
Standing at my narrow bed.

Only, of your tenderness,
  Pray a little prayer at night.
    Say: "I have forgiven now—
    I, so weak and sad; O Thou,
  Wreathed in thunder, robed in light,
Surely Thou wilt do no less."

AFTER A SPANISH PROVERB

Oh, mercifullest one of all,
  Oh, generous as dear,
None lived so lowly, none so small,
  Thou couldst withhold thy tear:

How swift, in pure compassion,
  How meek in charity,
To offer friendship to the one
  Who begged but love of thee!

Oh, gentle word, and sweetest said!
  Oh, tender hand, and first
To hold the warm, delicious bread
  To lips burned black of thirst.

THE FLAW IN PAGANISM

Drink and dance and laugh and lie,
   Love, the reeling midnight through,
For tomorrow we shall die!
   (But, alas, we never do.)

THE DANGER OF
WRITING DEFIANT VERSE

And now I have another lad!
    No longer need you tell
How all my nights are slow and sad
    For loving you too well.

His ways are not your wicked ways,
    He's not the like of you.
He treads his path of reckoned days,
    A sober man, and true.

They'll never see him in the town,
    Another on his knee.
He'd cut his laden orchards down,
    If that would pleasure me.

He'd give his blood to paint my lips
    If I should wish them red.
He prays to touch my finger-tips
    Or stroke my prideful head.

He never weaves a glinting lie,
    Or brags the hearts he'll keep.
I have forgotten how to sigh—
    Remembered how to sleep.

He's none to kiss away my mind—
　A slower way is his.
Oh, Lord! On reading this, I find
　A silly lot he is.

DISTANCE

Were you to cross the world, my dear,
   To work or love or fight,
I could be calm and wistful here,
   And close my eyes at night.

It were a sweet and gallant pain
   To be a sea apart;
But, oh, to have you down the lane
   Is bitter to my heart.

THE EVENING PRIMROSE

You know the bloom, unearthly white,
That none has seen by morning light—
The tender moon, alone, may bare
Its beauty to the secret air.
Who'd venture past its dark retreat
Must kneel, for holy things and sweet.
That blossom, mystically blown,
No man may gather for his own
Nor touch it, lest it droop and fall. . . .
Oh, I am not like that at all!

SANCTUARY

My land is bare of chattering folk;
    The clouds are low along the ridges,
And sweet's the air with curly smoke
    From all my burning bridges.

CHERRY WHITE

I never see that prettiest thing—
A cherry bough gone white with Spring—
But what I think, "How gay 'twould be
To hang me from a flowering tree."

SALOME'S DANCING-LESSON

She that begs a little boon
   (*Heel and toe! Heel and toe!*)
Little gets—and nothing, soon.
   (*No, no, no! No, no, no!*)
She that calls for costly things
Priceless finds her offerings—
What's impossible to kings?
   (*Heel and toe! Heel and toe!*)

Kings are shaped as other men.
   (*Step and turn! Step and turn!*)
Ask what none may ask again.
   (*Will you learn? Will you learn?*)
Lovers whine, and kisses pall,
Jewels tarnish, kingdoms fall—
Death's the rarest prize of all!
   (*Step and turn! Step and turn!*)

Veils are woven to be dropped.
   (*One, two, three! One, two, three!*)
Aging eyes are slowest stopped.
   (*Quietly! Quietly!*)
She whose body's young and cool
Has no need of dancing-school—
Scratch a king and find a fool!
   (*One, two, three! One, two, three!*)

MY OWN

Then let them point my every tear,
   And let them mock and moan;
Another week, another year,
   And I'll be with my own

Who slumber now by night and day
   In fields of level brown;
Whose hearts within their breasts were clay
   Before they laid them down.

SOLACE

There was a rose that faded young;
I saw its shattered beauty hung
   Upon a broken stem.
I heard them say, "What need to care
With roses budding everywhere?"
   I did not answer them.

There was a bird, brought down to die;
They said, "A hundred fill the sky—
   What reason to be sad?"
There was a girl, whose lover fled;
I did not wait, the while they said,
   "There's many another lad."

LITTLE WORDS

When you are gone, there is nor bloom nor leaf,
 Nor singing sea at night, nor silver birds;
And I can only stare, and shape my grief
 In little words.

I cannot conjure loveliness, to drown
 The bitter woe that racks my cords apart.
The weary pen that sets my sorrow down
 Feeds at my heart.

There is no mercy in the shifting year,
 No beauty wraps me tenderly about.
I turn to little words—so you, my dear,
 Can spell them out.

ORNITHOLOGY FOR BEGINNERS

The bird that feeds from off my palm
Is sleek, affectionate, and calm,
But double, to me, is worth the thrush
A-flickering in the elder-bush.

GARDEN-SPOT

God's acre was her garden-spot, she said;
   She sat there often, of the Summer days,
Little and slim and sweet, among the dead,
   Her hair a fable in the leveled rays.

She turned the fading wreath, the rusted cross,
   And knelt to coax about the wiry stem.
I see her gentle fingers on the moss
   Now it is anguish to remember them.

And once I saw her weeping, when she rose
   And walked a way and turned to look around·
The quick and envious tears of one that knows
   She shall not lie in consecrated ground.

TOMBSTONES IN THE STARLIGHT

I. THE MINOR POET

His little trills and chirpings were his best.
    No music like the nightingale's was born
Within his throat; but he, too, laid his breast
    Upon a thorn.

II. THE PRETTY LADY

She hated bleak and wintry things alone.
    All that was warm and quick, she loved too well-
A light, a flame, a heart against her own;
    It is forever bitter cold, in Hell.

III. THE VERY RICH MAN

He'd have the best, and that was none too good;
    No barrier could hold, before his terms.
He lies below, correct in cypress wood,
    And entertains the most exclusive worms.

IV. THE FISHERWOMAN

The man she had was kind and clean
    And well enough for every day,
But, oh, dear friends, you should have seen
    The one that got away!

V. THE CRUSADER

Arrived in Heaven, when his sands were run,
   He seized a quill, and sat him down to tell
The local press that something should be done
   About that noisy nuisance, Gabriel.

VI. THE ACTRESS

Her name, cut clear upon this marble cross,
   Shines, as it shone when she was still on earth;
While tenderly the mild, agreeable moss
   Obscures the figures of her date of birth.

THE LITTLE OLD LADY IN
LAVENDER SILK

I was seventy-seven, come August,
  I shall shortly be losing my bloom;
I've experienced zephyr and raw gust
  And (symbolical) flood and simoom.

When you come to this time of abatement,
  To this passing from Summer to Fall,
It is manners to issue a statement
  As to what you got out of it all.

So I'll say, though reflection unnerves me
  And pronouncements I dodge as I can,
That I think (if my memory serves me)
  There was nothing more fun than a man!

In my youth, when the crescent was too wan
  To embarrass with beams from above,   .
By the aid of some local Don Juan
  I fell into the habit of love.

And I learned how to kiss and be merry—an
  Education left better unsung.
My neglect of the waters Pierian
  Was a scandal, when Grandma was young.

Though the shabby unbalanced the splendid,
  And the bitter outmeasured the sweet,
I should certainly do as I then did,
  Were I given the chance to repeat.

For contrition is hollow and wraithful,
  And regret is no part of my plan,
And I think (if my memory's faithful)
  There was nothing more fun than a man!

VERS DÉMODÉ

For one, the amaryllis and the rose;
  The poppy, sweet as never lilies are;
The ripen'd vine, that beckons as it blows;
  The dancing star.

For one, the trodden rosemary and rue;
  The bowl, dipt ever in the purple stream.
And, for the other one, a fairer due—
  Sleep, and no dream.

SONNET FOR THE END OF A SEQUENCE

So take my vows and scatter them to sea;
Who swears the sweetest is no more than human.
And say no kinder words than these of me:
"Ever she longed for peace, but was a woman!
And thus they are, whose silly female dust
Needs little enough to clutter it and bind it,
Who meet a slanted gaze, and ever must
Go build themselves a soul to dwell behind it."

For now I am my own again, my friend!
This scar but points the whiteness of my breast;
This frenzy, like its betters, spins an end,
And now I am my own. And that is best.
Therefore, I am immeasurably grateful
To you, for proving shallow, false, and hateful.

THE APPLE TREE

When first we saw the apple tree
　　The boughs were dark and straight,
But never grief to give had we,
　　Though Spring delayed so late.

When last I came away from there
　　The boughs were heavy hung,
But little grief had I to spare
　　For Summer, perished young.

ISEULT OF BRITTANY

So delicate my hands, and long,
    They might have been my pride.
And there were those to make them song
    Who for their touch had died.

Too frail to cup a heart within,
    Too soft to hold the free—
How long these lovely hands have been
    A bitterness to me!

'STAR LIGHT, STAR BRIGHT—'

Star, that gives a gracious dole,
    What am I to choose?
Oh, will it be a shriven soul,
    Or little buckled shoes?

Shall I wish a wedding-ring,
    Bright and thin and round,
Or plead you send me covering—
    A newly spaded mound?

Gentle beam, shall I implore
    Gold, or sailing-ships,
Or beg I hate forevermore
    A pair of lying lips?

Swing you low or high away,
    Burn you hot or dim;
My only wish I dare not say—
    Lest you should grant me him.

THE SEA

Who lay against the sea, and fled,
   Who lightly loved the wave,
Shall never know, when he is dead,
   A cool and murmurous grave.

But in a shallow pit shall rest
   For all eternity,
And bear the earth upon the breast
   That once had worn the sea.

GUINEVERE AT HER FIRESIDE

A nobler king had never breath—
    I say it now, and said it then.
Who weds with such is wed till death
    And wedded stays in Heaven. Amen.

(And oh, the shirts of linen-lawn,
    And all the armor, tagged and tied,
And church on Sundays, dusk and dawn,
    And bed a thing to kneel beside!)

The bravest one stood tall above
    The rest, and watched me as a light.
I heard and heard them talk of love;
    I'd naught to do but think, at night.

The bravest man has littlest brains;
    That chalky fool from Astolat
With all her dying and her pains!—
    Thank God, I helped him over that.

I found him not unfair to see—
    I like a man with peppered hair!
And thus it came about. Ah, me,
    Tristram was busied otherwhere. . . .

A nobler king had never breath—
    I say it now, and said it then.
Who weds with such is wed till death
    And wedded stays in Heaven. Amen.

TRANSITION

Too long and quickly have I lived to vow
   The woe that stretches me shall never wane,
   Too often seen the end of endless pain
To swear that peace no more shall cool my brow.
I know, I know—again the shriveled bough
   Will burgeon sweetly in the gentle rain,
   And these hard lands be quivering with grain—
I tell you only: it is Winter now.

What if I know, before the Summer goes
Where dwelt this bitter frenzy shall be rest?
What is it now, that June shall surely bring
New promise, with the swallow and the rose?
My heart is water, that I first must breast
The terrible, slow loveliness of Spring.

S ON READING TOO MANY POETS

Roses, rooted warm in earth,
  Bud in rhyme, another age;
Lilies know a ghostly birth
  Strewn along a patterned page;
Golden lad and chimbley sweep
Die; and so their song shall keep.

Wind that in Arcadia starts
  In and out a couplet plays;
And the drums of bitter hearts
  Beat the measure of a phrase.
Sweets and woes but come to print
Quae cum ita sint.

FROM A LETTER FROM LESBIA

... So, praise the gods, at last he's away!
   And let me tend you this advice, my dear:
Take any lover that you will, or may,
   Except a poet. All of them are queer.

It's just the same—a quarrel or a kiss
   Is but a tune to play upon his pipe.
He's always hymning that or wailing this;
   Myself, I much prefer the business type.

That thing he wrote, the time the sparrow died—
   (Oh, most unpleasant—gloomy, tedious words!)
I called it sweet, and made believe I cried;
   The stupid fool! I've always hated birds. ...

BALLADE OF UNFORTUNATE MAMMALS

Love is sharper than stones or sticks;
  Lone as the sea, and deeper blue;
Loud in the night as a clock that ticks;
  Longer-lived than the Wandering Jew.
Show me a love was done and through,
  Tell me a kiss escaped its debt!
Son, to your death you'll pay your due—
  Women and elephants never forget.

Ever a man, alas, would mix,
  Ever a man, heigh-ho, must woo;
So he's left in the world-old fix,
  Thus is furthered the sale of rue.
Son, your chances are thin and few—
  Won't you ponder, before you're set?
Shoot if you must, but hold in view
  Women and elephants never forget.

Down from Cæsar past Joynson-Hicks
  Echoes the warning, ever new:
Though they're trained to amusing tricks,
  Gentler, they, than the pigeon's coo,
Careful, son, of the cursèd two—
  Either one is a dangerous pet;
Natural history proves it true—
  Women and elephants never forget.

L'ENVOI

Prince, a precept I'd leave for you,
    Coined in Eden, existing yet:
Skirt the parlor, and shun the zoo—
    Women and elephants never forget.

PURPOSELY UNGRAMMATICAL
LOVE SONG

There's many and many, and not so far,
   Is willing to dry my tears away;
There's many to tell me what you are,
   And never a lie to all they say.

It's little the good to hide my head,
   It's never the use to bar my door;
There's many as counts the tears I shed,
   There's mourning hearts for my heart is sore.

There's honester eyes than your blue eyes,
   There's better a mile than such as you.
But when did I say that I was wise,
   And when did I hope that you were true?

PRAYER FOR A NEW MOTHER

The things she knew, let her forget again—
  The voices in the sky, the fear, the cold,
The gaping shepherds, and the queer old men
  Piling their clumsy gifts of foreign gold.

Let her have laughter with her little one;
  Teach her the endless, tuneless songs to sing;
Grant her her right to whisper to her son
  The foolish names one dare not call a king.

Keep from her dreams the rumble of a crowd,
  The smell of rough-cut wood, the trail of red,
The thick and chilly whiteness of the shroud
  That wraps the strange new body of the dead.

Ah, let her go, kind Lord, where mothers go
  And boast his pretty words and ways, and plan
The proud and happy years that they shall know
  Together, when her son is grown a man.

MIDNIGHT

The stars are soft as flowers, and as near;
  The hills are webs of shadow, slowly spun;
No separate leaf or single blade is here—
  All blend to one.

No moonbeam cuts the air; a sapphire light
  Rolls lazily, and slips again to rest.
There is no edgèd thing in all this night,
  Save in my breast.

NINON DE LENCLOS,
ON HER LAST BIRTHDAY

So let me have the rouge again,
    And comb my hair the curly way.
The poor young men, the dear young men—
    They'll all be here by noon today.

And I shall wear the blue, I think—
    They beg to touch its rippled lace;
Or do they love me best in pink,
    So sweetly flattering the face?

And are you sure my eyes are bright,
    And is it true my cheek is clear?
Young what's-his-name stayed half the night;
    He vows to cut his throat, poor dear!

So bring my scarlet slippers, then,
    And fetch the powder-puff to me.
The dear young men, the poor young men—
    They think I'm only seventy!

ULTIMATUM

I'm wearied of wearying love, my friend,
  Of worry and strain and doubt;
Before we begin, let us view the end,
  And maybe I'll do without.
There's never the pang that was worth the tear,
  And toss in the night I won't—
So either you do or you don't, my dear,
  Either you do or you don't!

The table is ready, so lay your cards
  And if they should augur pain,
I'll tender you ever my kind regards
  And run for the fastest train.
I haven't the will to be spent and sad;
  My heart's to be gay and true—
Then either you don't or you do, my lad,
  Either you don't or you do!

OF A WOMAN, DEAD YOUNG

(J. H., 1905–1930)

If she had been beautiful, even,
Or wiser than women about her,
Or had moved with a certain defiance;
If she had had sons at her sides,
And she with her hands on their shoulders,
Sons, to make troubled the Gods—
But where was there wonder in her?
What had she, better or eviler,
Whose days were a pattering of peas
From the pod to the bowl in her lap?

That the pine tree is blasted by lightning,
And the bowlder split raw from the mountain,
And the river dried short in its rushing—
That I can know, and be humble.
But that They who have trodden the stars
Should turn from Their echoing highway
To trample a daisy, unnoticed
In a field full of small, open flowers—
Where is Their triumph in that?
Where is Their pride, and Their vengeance?

THE WILLOW

On sweet young earth where the myrtle presses,
    Long we lay, when the May was new;
The willow was winding the moon in her tresses,
    The bud of the rose was told with dew.

And now on the brittle ground I'm lying,
    Screaming to die with the dead year's dead;
The stem of the rose is black and drying,
    The willow is tossing the wind from her head.

SONNET ON AN ALPINE NIGHT

My hand, a little raised, might press a star;
Where I may look, the frosted peaks are spun,
So shaped before Olympus was begun,
Spanned each to each, now, by a silver bar.
Thus to face Beauty have I traveled far,
But now, as if around my heart were run
Hard, lacing fingers, so I stand undone.
Of all my tears, the bitterest these are.

Who humbly followed Beauty all her ways,
Begging the brambles that her robe had passed,
Crying her name in corridors of stone,
That day shall know his weariedest of days—
When Beauty, still and suppliant at last,
Does not suffice him, once they are alone.

BALLADE OF A TALKED-OFF EAR

Daily I listen to wonder and woe,
Nightly I hearken to knave or to ace,
Telling me stories of lava and snow,
Delicate fables of ribbon and lace,
Tales of the quarry, the kill, the chase,
Longer than heaven and duller than hell—
Never you blame me, who cry my case:
"Poets alone should kiss and tell!"

Dumbly I hear what I never should know,
Gently I counsel of pride and of grace;
Into minutiæ gayly they go,
Telling the name and the time and the place.
Cede them your silence and grant them space—
Who tenders an inch shall be raped of an ell!
Sympathy's ever the boaster's brace;
Poets alone should kiss and tell.

Why am I tithed what I never did owe?
Choked with vicarious saffron and mace?
Weary my lids, and my fingers are slow—
Gentlemen, damn you, you've halted my pace.
Only the lads of the cursèd race,
Only the knights of the desolate spell,
May point me the lines the blood-drops trace—
Poets alone should kiss and tell.

L'ENVOI

Prince or commoner, tenor or bass,
Painter or plumber or never-do-well,
Do me a favor and shut your face—
Poets alone should kiss and tell.

REQUIESCAT

Tonight my love is sleeping cold
   Where none may see and none shall pass.
The daisies quicken in the mold,
   And richer fares the meadow grass.

The warding cypress pleads the skies,
   The mound goes level in the rain.
My love all cold and silent lies—
   Pray God it will not rise again!

SWEET VIOLETS

You are brief and frail and blue—
Little sisters, I am, too.
You are Heaven's masterpieces—
Little loves, the likeness ceases.

PROLOGUE TO A SAGA

Maidens, gather not the yew,
  Leave the glossy myrtle sleeping;
Any lad was born untrue,
  Never a one is fit your weeping.

Pretty dears, your tumult cease;
  Love's a fardel, burthening double.
Clear your hearts, and have you peace—
  Gangway, girls: I'll show you trouble.

SUMMARY

Every love's the love before
    In a duller dress.
That's the measure of my lore—
    Here's my bitterness:
Would I knew a little more,
    Or very much less!

SIGHT

Unseemly are the open eyes
 That watch the midnight sheep,
That look upon the secret skies
 Nor close, abashed, in sleep;

That see the dawn drag in, unbidden,
 To birth another day—
Oh, better far their gaze were hidden
 Below the decent clay.

THE LADY'S REWARD

Lady, lady, never start
Conversation toward your heart;
Keep your pretty words serene;
Never murmur what you mean.
Show yourself, by word and look,
Swift and shallow as a brook.
Be as cool and quick to go
As a drop of April snow;
Be as delicate and gay
As a cherry flower in May.
Lady, lady, never speak
Of the tears that burn your cheek—
She will never win him, whose
Words had shown she feared to lose.
Be you wise and never sad,
You will get your lovely lad.
Never serious be, nor true,
And your wish will come to you—
And if that makes you happy, kid,
You'll be the first it ever did.

PRISONER

Long I fought the driving lists,
    Plume a-stream and armor clanging;
Link on link, between my wrists,
    Now my heavy freedom's hanging.

TEMPS PERDU

I never may turn the loop of a road
   Where sudden, ahead, the sea is lying,
But my heart drags down with an ancient load—
   My heart, that a second before was flying.

I never behold the quivering rain—
   And sweeter the rain than a lover to me—
But my heart is wild in my breast with pain;
   My heart, that was tapping contentedly.

There's never a rose spreads new at my door
   Nor a strange bird crosses the moon at night
But I know I have known its beauty before,
   And a terrible sorrow along with the sight.

The look of a laurel tree birthed for May
   Or a sycamore bared for a new November
Is as old and as sad as my furtherest day—
   What is it, what is it, I almost remember?

AUTUMN VALENTINE

In May my heart was breaking—
  Oh, wide the wound, and deep!
And bitter it beat at waking,
  And sore it split in sleep.

And when it came November,
  I sought my heart, and sighed,
"Poor thing, do you remember?"
  "What heart was that?" it cried.

INDEX OF
FIRST LINES

INDEX OF FIRST LINES

INDEX OF FIRST LINES

[206]

[210]

CPSIA information can be obtained at www.ICGtesting.com
Printed in the USA
BVOW01s1449061213

338393BV00006B/279/P